Contents

2	Your child and literacy	
3	How to use this book	
4-5	The Alphabet	Letter names and sounds
6-7	Find the Sound	Final and initial letter sounds
8-9	Practise Your Sounds	Word-building
10-11	Starting and Stopping	Capital letters and full stops
12-13	My Diary	Planning and sequencing
14-15	Beginning, Middle and End	Story structure and sequencing
16-17	Rhyme	Rhyming words
18-19	Practise Your Sounds More	Word-building
20-21	Postcards	Creative writing
22-23	Sentence Maker	Simple sentence structure
24-25	Speech Bubbles	Characters and expression
26-27	Clap with Words	Syllables
28-29	Practise Your Sounds Again	Word-building
30-31	Vowels	Vowels as medial sounds
32-33	Silly Sentences	Learning difficult spellings
34-35	Look, Say, Cover, Write, Check	Learning to spell
36-37	New Sentences	Simple sentence structure
38-39	In the Past	The past tense
40	Helping your child	

Pull-out pages

The ot Pot and at Hat	Word endings
Alphabetical Houses	Alphabetical order
Castle Adventure Book	Creative writing

Your child and literacy

From September 1998, after a very successful trial year, most primary schools must carry out a daily hour of literacy, to meet new standards set by the government.

What is literacy?
According to the published guidelines, primary pupils should be able to:
- read, write and spell confidently;
- correct their own mistakes;
- write fluently and legibly;
- have a growing vocabulary;
- write in a variety of styles e.g. stories and poetry;
- use non-fiction;
- discuss their reading and writing;
- develop their imagination through books.

Literacy at Key Stage 1
At Key Stage 1 (ages 4–7), the literacy hour will aim to develop the following skills:
- phonics and spelling;
- word recognition;
- handwriting;
- vocabulary;
- grammar;
- reading and writing fiction, poetry and non-fiction.

The literacy hour
The daily 60 minutes is divided into 4 main sections:
1. Whole class work (15 minutes), during which the children and teacher share a text.
2. Whole class work (15 minutes), focusing on words.
3. Group and individual work (20 minutes), when the children are divided into ability groups and the teacher works with certain groups while the others work independently.
4. Whole class work (10 minutes) to discuss the work covered in the lesson.

Your child's teacher will explain the hour to you in detail, and may invite parents to help with reading.

Turn to page 40 for ways to help your child's writing.

How to use this book

As children progress through the Key Stage 1 years (ages 4–7), they acquire many reading, writing and mathematics skills which prepare for further education at Key Stage 2 and beyond.

Each book in this series is organised into 18 activity pages which provide practice in the skills your child will be developing at school.

Activities: Your child should use a pencil to fill in the activity pages. Take time to read any instructions together and to discuss the pictures.

Character: Gives tips, advice and key words.

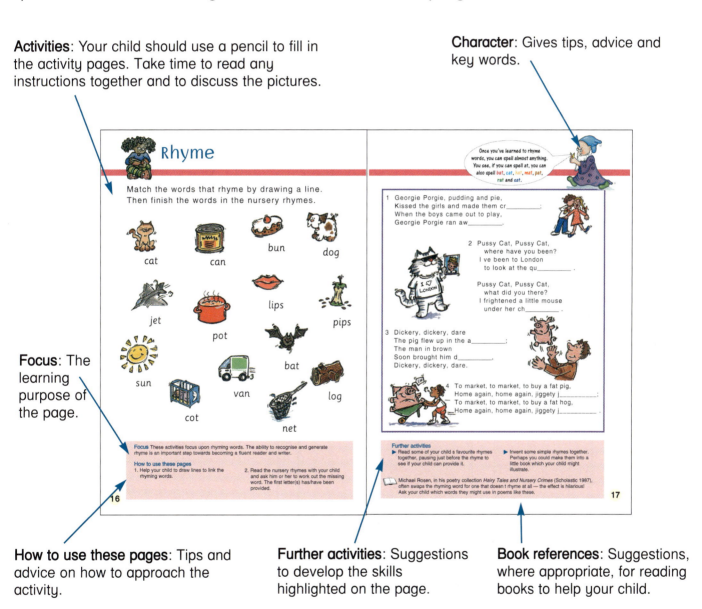

Focus: The learning purpose of the page.

How to use these pages: Tips and advice on how to approach the activity.

Further activities: Suggestions to develop the skills highlighted on the page.

Book references: Suggestions, where appropriate, for reading books to help your child.

Remember, learning should be enjoyable. Work at your child's pace and emphasise successes rather than failures.

And finally, have fun!

The Alphabet

Draw an object which starts with each letter of the alphabet.

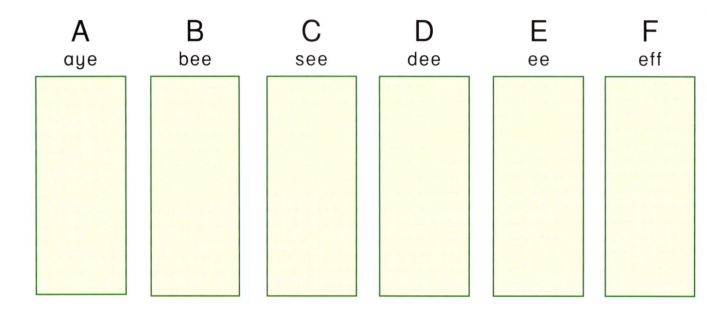

A	B	C	D	E	F
aye	bee	see	dee	ee	eff

N	O	P	Q	R	S	T
en	owe	pee	kyew	are	ess	tee

Focus These activities encourage your child to understand letter names (above the picture boxes) and alphabetical order.

How to use these pages
1. With your child, point at the letter names, saying them as you go.
2. Ask your child to draw a picture in each box of an object beginning with the initial letter.

Old magazines, comics and newspapers will give you lots of ideas for writing.

G	H	I	J	K	L	M
jee	aitch	eye	jay	kay	ell	em

U	V	W	X	Y	Z
ewe	vee	double u	ex	why	zed

Further activities
- Help your child to write the words beneath the pictures, highlighting the initial sound in a separate colour.
- Draw a larger version of the alphabet grid. Ask your child to find magazine pictures which correspond to the initial letter, cut them out and stick them in the boxes. This makes a colourful mural.
- Draw the same 26 pictures onto cards and, on another set of 26 cards, write the corresponding words. Mix them up and ask your child to try to match them.

Find the Sound

Fill in the missing letters.

we___

woo___

ba___

ma___

dru___

foo___

Focus These activities develop your child's phonic skills by encouraging him or her to listen out for final, as well as initial, letter sounds.

How to use these pages
1. Ask your child what the pictures represent and say what each object is aloud.
2. One word at a time, help your child to fill in the missing sound at the end of the word.

Say the words slowly to yourself, and stop at the very last sound. Listen carefully to the last sound. Can you recognise it?

trai___

sn___

ha___

fo___

ba___

Further activities

▶ Choose five things you can see nearby. Ask your child to name these things, and to say the final sound in each word. (Note: be sure to choose objects which do not end with a silent letter, e.g. house.)

▶ Draw the above pictures onto cards. Beneath, write the corresponding word, but not the final sound. On separate cards, write the final sounds. Ask your child to match the cards.

The *Spot* series by Eric Hill (various publishers) contains very simple vocabulary. Read one to your child and ask him or her to listen out for the final sounds of words.

Practise Your Sounds

Match the word to the picture by drawing a line.

Focus These activities help to develop your child's word-building skills. They also reinforce correct letter formation.

How to use these pages
1. Read the words in the boxes with your child and match them to the corresponding picture by drawing a line. The alphabet key may help as a prompt.
2. When your child has traced over the shaded words (begin each letter at the heavy dot), ask him or her to copy the words beneath, between the lines.

To write your letters, start on the dots.

Now copy out the words:

arm

butterfly

card

dragon

eye

frog

glove

horse

a b c d e f g h i j k l m n o p q r s t u v w x y z

Further activities
▶ Ask your child to practise spelling these words by writing them in the air with his or her finger; writing them on your back to see if you can guess which word is being written; using the 'look, say, cover, write, check' method (see pages 34-35).

▶ Look these words up in a children's dictionary, pointing out that the dictionary is ordered alphabetically.
▶ Help your child to invent six sentences of his or her own, each one containing one of the above words.

Starting and Stopping

Can you work out where the capital letters and full stops should go? Try to read the passage aloud.

once upon a time, a little girl went to visit her grandma who lived in the forest the girl wore a red cloak with a red hood people called her little red riding hood as she was walking through the forest, a wolf watched her from behind a tree he was feeling hungry so he followed little red riding hood to her grandma's house and quickly entered through the back door as little red riding hood walked up the path, the wolf pulled little red riding hood's grandma out of her bed he locked her in the cupboard, put on her clothes and got into bed just at that moment little red riding hood knocked at the front door…

Now see if you were right by reading this version with capital letters and full stops.

Once upon a time, a little girl went to visit her grandma who lived in the forest. The girl wore a red cloak with a red hood. People called her Little Red Riding Hood. As she was walking through the forest, a wolf watched her from behind a tree. He was feeling hungry so he followed Little Red Riding Hood to her Grandma's house and quickly entered through the back door. As Little Red Riding Hood walked up the path, the wolf pulled Little Red Riding Hood's Grandma out of her bed. He locked her in the cupboard, put on her clothes and got into bed. Just at that moment Little Red Riding Hood knocked at the front door…

Focus These activities draw your child's attention to the purpose of capital letters and punctuation.

How to use these pages
1. Read the version of *Little Red Riding Hood* without punctuation. Encourage your child to work out where the sentences begin and end. Check by looking at the punctuated version beneath. Explain that full stops allow you to stop or to take a breath.
2. Next, match the text to the pictures. Help your child to write the corresponding sentences beneath the pictures.

> Sentences are very difficult to read without capital letters and full stops. Try to write sentences for the pictures below.

_____

_____

_____

_____

_____

_____

_____

_____

_____

_____

_____

_____

Further activities

▶ Ask your child to continue the story of *Little Red Riding Hood* orally. Ask your child to look up and smile each time he or she comes to the end of a sentence – this is great fun!

▶ Ask your child to write the end of the story, or help by acting as scribe, encouraging him or her to punctuate correctly.

Read books with your child which contain only one sentence per page, for example *Spot's First Walk* by Eric Hill (Heinemann, 1981). Together with your child, write your own 'one sentence per page' book, with illustrations.

My Diary

For four days, write down all the things that happen to you. Draw a picture to go with each day.

Day 1
_____

_____

_____

_____

_____

Day 3
_____

_____

_____

_____

_____

Focus These activities will develop your child's ability to sequence and plan his or her writing.

How to use these pages
1. Make sure your child writes the day of the week next to the date, not forgetting the capital letters.
2. Talk about the order in which things happened with your child, and ask him or her to write a brief account on the lines provided. Your child may then draw an appropriate picture in each box.

Many people record their lives in diaries. Samuel Pepys wrote a famous diary from 1660-1669, in which he described many historic events.

Day 2 _____

_____

_____

_____

_____

_____

Day 4 _____

_____

_____

_____

_____

_____

_____

Further activities

▶ Ask your child to keep a weekend diary in which he or she could draw pictures, collect souvenirs (e.g. bus tickets, postcards) and write simple accounts of events.

▶ Buy a calendar for your child, on which he or she may record important occasions, e.g. birthdays, holidays, etc.

 Numerous picture books tell sequenced stories; good examples are *Rosie's Walk* by Pat Hutchins (Bodley Head, 1968) or *Mr Gumpy's Outing* by John Burningham (Cape, 1970). Encourage your child to tell or write the story in his or her own words.

Beginning, Middle

Read the **beginning** of the story, play the game in the **middle**, then read the **end**.

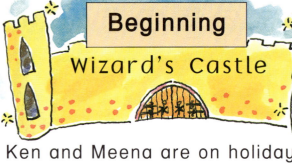

Beginning

Wizard's Castle

Middle

Faraway Forest
Toss a coin to find a way to the wand.

Ken and Meena are on holiday at Bathing Beach. One day, they decide to go for a walk. They walk for an hour, until they reach a forest. They realise they are lost! After a while, they come to the Word Wizard's castle. They knock at the door. Word Wizard is happy to help Ken and Meena get back to Bathing Beach, but first he must find his wand which he has lost somewhere in Faraway Forest. Now play the game to see if you can you help them to find the wand...

Focus These activities concentrate on story structure and sequencing.

How to use these pages
1. Read the beginning (Wizard's Castle) of the story with your child.
2. When you come to the game (Faraway Forest) in the middle section, you and your child can take turns to toss a coin and move forwards (or backwards) according to the arrows.
3. When one of you arrives at the final square, you should finish by reading the end section (Bathing Beach) of the story.

and End

A good story has a beginning which sets the scene, a middle where the action happens, and an end to complete the story.

End

Bathing Beach

So, after carefully removing the wand from the hedgehog's prickles, the Word Wizard says the magic words and Ken and Meena find themselves back on Bathing Beach.

"Would you both like a candy floss?" asks the Word Wizard. "Yes please, Wiz!" shout Ken and Meena. So the Word Wizard waves his wand at the candy floss machine and all three watch as the candy floss grows.

"That's the best use I've ever made of my wand," says the Word Wizard as they all munch away happily at the fluffy pink sugar.

"Thanks, Wiz," say Ken and Meena.

Further activities
▶ Ask your child to think of a different ending to the story. He or she might like to draw a picture to accompany the new ending.

▶ Plan another story with your child, using the headings 'beginning', 'middle' and 'end'. You could then write it for your child and turn it into a book for him or her.

Read the *Bad-tempered Ladybird* by Eric Carle (Hamish Hamilton 1978). This is about the adventures of a ladybird who thinks he is braver than he is. Write 'A Day in the Life' of your own child, with time-referenced events.

Rhyme

Match the words that rhyme by drawing a line.
Then finish the words in the nursery rhymes.

Focus These activities focus upon rhyming words. The ability to recognise and generate rhyme is an important step towards becoming a fluent reader and writer.

How to use these pages
1. Help your child to draw lines to link the rhyming words.
2. Read the nursery rhymes with your child and ask him or her to work out the missing word. The first letter(s) has/have been provided.

Once you've learned to rhyme words, you can spell almost anything. You see, if you can spell at, you can also spell bat, cat, hat, mat, pat, rat and sat.

1   Georgie Porgie, pudding and pie,
    Kissed the girls and made them cr_____;
    When the boys came out to play,
    Georgie Porgie ran aw_____.

2   Pussy Cat, Pussy Cat,
        where have you been?
    "I've been to London
        to look at the qu_____."

    Pussy Cat, Pussy Cat,
        what did you there?
    "I frightened a little mouse
        under her ch_____."

3   Dickery, dickery, dare
    The pig flew up in the a_____;
    The man in brown
    Soon brought him d_____,
    Dickery, dickery, dare.

4   To market, to market, to buy a fat pig,
    Home again, home again, jiggety j_____;
    To market, to market, to buy a fat hog,
    Home again, home again, jiggety j_____.

Further activities

▶ Read some of your child's favourite rhymes together, pausing just before the rhyme to see if your child can provide it.

▶ Invent some simple rhymes together. Perhaps you could make them into a little book which your child might illustrate.

Michael Rosen, in his poetry collection *Hairy Tales and Nursery Crimes* (Scholastic 1987), often swaps the rhyming word for one that doesn't rhyme at all – the effect is hilarious! Ask your child which words they might use in poems like these.

Practise Your Sounds

Match the word to the picture by drawing a line.

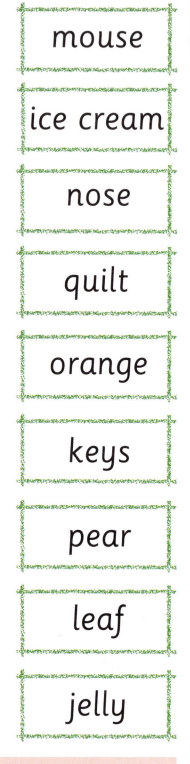

Focus These activities help to develop your child's word-building skills. They also reinforce correct letter formation.

How to use these pages
1. Read the words in the boxes with your child and match them to the corresponding picture by drawing a line. The alphabet may provide a prompt.
2. When your child has traced over the shaded words (begin each letter at the heavy dot), ask him or her to copy the words beneath, between the lines.

More

Now trace over the words, and then try to write them on your own.

Now copy out the words:

ice cream

jelly

keys

leaf

mouse

nose

orange

pear

quilt

a b c d e f g h **i j k l m n o p q** r s t u v w x y z

Further activities
▶ Ask your child to practise spelling these words by writing them in the air with his or her finger; writing them on to your back with his or her finger to see if you can guess which word is being written; using the 'look, say, cover, write, check' method (see pages 34-35).

▶ Help your child to invent nine sentences, each one containing one of the above words.
▶ Write more words which begin with the same nine sounds.

Postcards

Read the postcard to Gabriella.

SPAIN

Dear Gabriella,

We're having a fantastic time in Spain. The sun is shining, the sea is warm, and the beach is sandy. We've been on lots of trips, too. See you soon!

Love from Grannie and Grandpa
xx　　xx

Gabriella Hitel,
40 Morady Road,
Waltham Abbey,
Essex

Focus These activities allow your child to write about personal events in a creative way. They also show how to write addresses.

How to use these pages
1. Look at the postcard above. What can your child see on the picture? Point out how the written side of a postcard is set out. If available, show your child some real postcards. What information can he or she find?
2. Ask your child to design and write a postcard on the blanks opposite.

Postcards are great fun to write. Send some to your friends, but remember to copy out the address properly.

Design and write your own postcard from your dream holiday place.

Further activities
- ▶ Help your child to send a real postcard to someone he or she knows.
- ▶ Make your own postcards by cutting out pictures from holiday brochures and sticking them on to blank postcards or plain pieces of card.
- ▶ Encourage your child to keep a scrapbook of postcards.

The Jolly Postman, *The Jolly Christmas Postman*, and *The Jolly Pocket Postman*, by Janet and Allan Ahlberg (Heinemann, 1986, 1991, 1995), provide numerous examples of how to write letters.

Sentence Maker

See how many sentences you can make using the following words.

we	to	and	park	nice
can	went	do	some	want
I	what	trees	the	eat
see	flowers	is	they	where
good	did	am	little	are

Focus These activities will help your child to recognise common words, and to learn about simple sentence structure.

How to use these pages
1. Read aloud all the words in the grid. Help your child to sequence these words in different ways to make simple sentences.
2. Help your child to write the sentences on the lines provided. Encourage your child to use capital letters and full stops.

Remember, sentences start with capital letters and end with full stops.

Write your sentences here.

Further activities
▶ Group the words into categories, according to their starting letter. Which letter group contains the most words?

▶ See how many of these words your child can spell. Make a note of the words which he or she finds difficult, and encourage your child to learn them using the 'look, say, cover, write, check' method on pages 34-35.

Speech Bubbles

Read the story and look at the pictures. Can you work out what the different characters are saying?

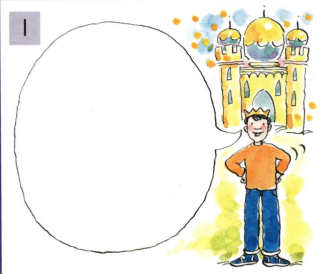

1. Once upon a time there lived a prince called Joshua, who was very handsome.

2. A witch lived nearby. She was so jealous of the prince's good looks that she turned him into a frog. He would only ever become a prince again if a princess were to fall in love with him.

5. The princess agreed, but she thought the frog was so ugly that she would not look at him. The next morning, the frog had disappeared.

6. As Laura played with her ball that same day, the frog appeared again, and saved the princess's ball from being lost. Again, he asked to spend the night in the castle.

Focus These activities encourage your child to think about how different fictional characters speak and, therefore, to read with expression.

How to use these pages
1. Read through the story with your child, paying special attention to the pictures.
2. Next, read the story one box at a time, and ask your child to guess what the characters might be saying. Your child may fill in the speech bubbles or you could act as scribe.
3. Finally, read the story again, but this time allowing time for your child to read the speech bubbles. Encourage your child to adopt particular voices for each specific character.

Now it's your turn to fill in the speech bubbles!

3 One day, a beautiful princess called Laura was bouncing her ball near the pond when, all of a sudden, it turned and bounced into the water.

4 At once an ugly frog jumped out from the pond, and offered to fetch Laura's ball – on the condition that she would let him stay in her castle for the night.

7 The next morning, the frog had disappeared once more. Princess Laura had grown fond of the frog by now, and began to cry.

8 Suddenly a handsome prince appeared. He told Princess Laura that her love had broken the wicked witch's spell and turned him from a frog back into a prince again.

Further activities
- Record the story onto tape, with your child saying the words in the speech bubbles.
- Take other favourite stories, and try to work out what different characters would say, and what voices they would use.
- Talk about how traditional fairy tales often include handsome princes, princesses, witches who cast spells, wise wizards etc.

 Read *The Tough Princess* by Martin Waddell (Walker Books, 1989). Some modern authors have taken the traditional style and made funny, more realistic stories.

Clap with Words

Look at this family at home. How many sounds are there in each name? And how many sounds are there in the other objects? Clap as you say them aloud.

Dad-dy   Mum-my   So-phie   Ja-cob   O-li-ver

ban-an-a

pic-ture

set-tee

chick-en

ta-ble

yog-hurt   lamp   to-ffee pu-dding

Focus These activities help to introduce your child to syllables.

How to use these pages

1. With your child, talk about how all words have different groups of sounds in them. Try clapping the rhythm of the words of objects nearby. Look at the picture above, and clap out the words as your child says them.

2. Mark in the syllables on the opposite page, following the example. Write the number of syllables in the box.

The different sounds in words are called syllables. In my name there is one syllable – **word** – then two syllables – **wiz-ard**.

Divide these words into syllables by drawing lines through each word.
Write the number of syllables in the box.

The first one has been done for you.

 d a f f / o / d i l 3

 b a b y

 r o c k i n g   h o r s e

 o c t o p u s

 r a d i o

Further activities
- On a piece of plain paper, draw three vertical columns, then help your child fill in the columns. In the first column write words of one syllable, in the second column write words of two syllables, and in the third column write words of three syllables.
- Play the game *Don't Clap This One Back* in which you clap different simple rhythms, and your child claps them back identically. However, when the rhythm clapped is that of *Don't Clap This One Back*, your child remains still. Take it in turns to be the 'clapper'. Try to trick each other!

Practise Your Sounds

Match the word to the picture by drawing a line.

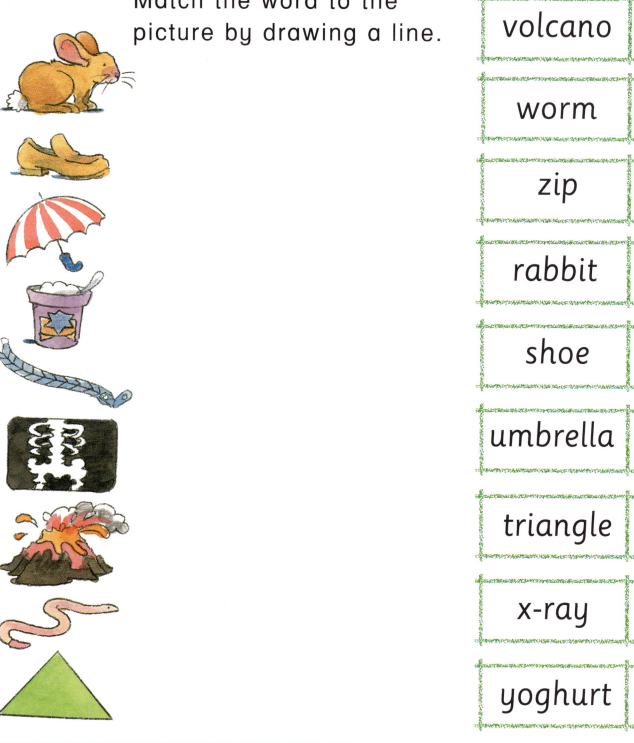

Focus These activities help to develop your child's word-building skills. They also reinforce correct letter formation.

How to use these pages
1. Read the words in the boxes with your child and match them to the corresponding picture by drawing a line. The alphabet key may act as a prompt.
2. When your child has traced over the shaded words (begin each letter at the heavy dot), ask him or her to copy the words directly beneath, between the lines.

Again

Can you remember how to write the letters, r, s, t, u, v, w, x, y, and z?

Now copy out the words:

rabbit

shoe

triangle

umbrella

volcano

worm

x-ray

yoghurt

zip

a b c d e f g h i j k l m n o p q r s t u v w x y z

Further activities
- Ask your child to practise spelling these words by writing them in the air with his or her finger; writing them on your back with his or her finger to see if you can guess which word is being written; using the 'look, say, cover, write, check' method (see pages 34-35).
- Help your child to write one or two sentences, which include all of the words listed above.
- Help your child to place the same nine words in alphabetical order.

Vowels

Find the missing vowel from the middle of these words.

c__t

ch__ps

b__tter

b__s

d__g

p__n

p__n

h__t

Focus These activities introduce your child to vowels as the medial sound in words.

How to use these pages
1. Talk with your child about the vowels – that there are five of them, the sounds they make, and that almost all words in the English language contain at least one of them.
2. Ask your child to name the pictures and to identify the missing sound.

Vowels are the letters **a**, **e**, **i**, **o** and **u**. You need them to make words.

m_p sw_m m_p

t_p c_t h_n

t_n f_sh

Further activities
- Write down several words for your child and see if he or she can tell you which words contain most vowels.
- Think of five words whose beginning sounds are vowels.
- With your child, try to find words which don't contain any vowels.

Silly Sentences

Look at the pictures and sentences below. If you take the first letter of each word and join them together, they spell another word. Can you find the new words?

Tables have eaten yoghurts.

Little insects kiss eggs.

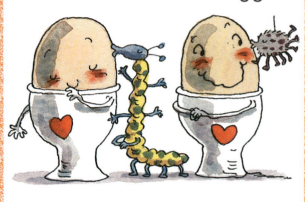

William hurls oranges.

Sad ants in dustbins.

Focus These activities help your child to find ways to learn difficult spellings.

How to use these pages

1. With your child, look at the pictures and read the accompanying sentences together. By taking the first letter of each word, work out which word the sentence helps you to spell.

2. Ask your child to write the word in the space below, paying attention to correct letter formation. (Note: this is only one way to practise spelling, and should not be relied upon alone.)

These silly sentences help me to spell difficult words. Which words do you find difficult?

Big elephants fall over red eggs.

Pretty leeks are yawning.

Cats are looking lovely.

Further activities

▶ Children love to make the sentences as silly as possible. Invent more silly sentences to help your child spell words which he or she finds particularly tricky.

▶ Make a 'silly sentences' book of these words, which your child can illustrate and keep as a personal word book to aid his or her own writing.

▶ Ask your child to make up sentences containing these words.

Look, Say, Cover,

The best way to learn your spellings is to look at them carefully, say the words, and then try to write them down.

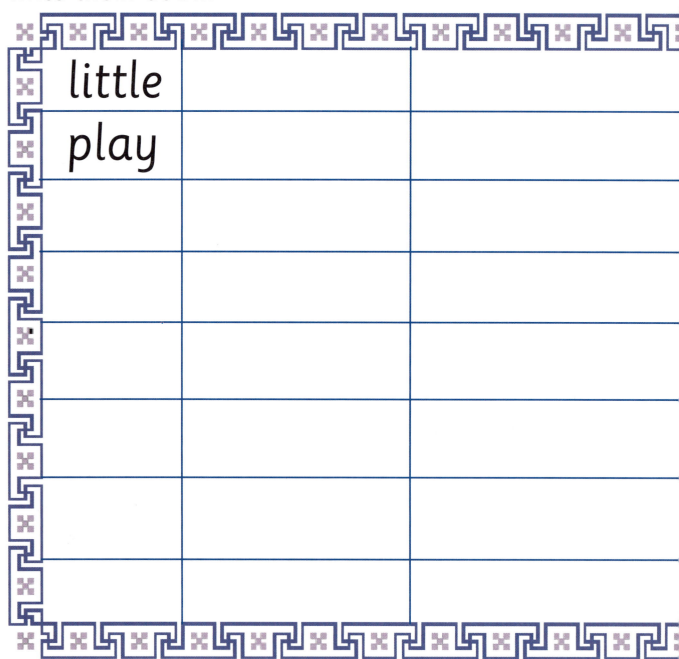

little

play

Focus These activities display the importance of the spoken word in learning to spell effectively.

How to use these pages
1. To learn to spell a word, write it for your child in the left-hand column, e.g. 'cat'. Your child should then look at it, say it aloud, cover it up, write it in the next box to the right and check it against the original.

2. Repeat this four times until all the boxes in a horizontal line are full. The word should now be firmly fixed in your child's memory. Do not attempt more than three new words at a time if your child is struggling.

Write, Check

Remember, when you're learning to spell a word, it is very important that you say it aloud first.

Further activities
- Each time your child needs to learn a new spelling, learn it in this way. You could make your own 'look, say, cover, write, check' sheets, and keep them in a file as a record.
- Ask your child to practise words by writing them with his or her finger in the air, or on someone's back – it's great fun!
- Together with your child, try to find patterns in spelling, e.g. 'How many words can you think of that end with -at, -ut, -on, -op?'

New Sentences

See how many sentences you can make using the following words.

he	hospital	are	café	you
to	dentist	him	on	go
is	tonic	she	coffee	shop
tea	the	has	gives	at
can	have	goes	her	it

Focus These activities will help your child to recognise common words, and to learn about simple sentence structure.

How to use these pages
1. Read aloud all the words in the grid. Help your child to sequence these words in different ways to make simple sentences.
2. Write the sentences on the lines provided. Encourage your child to use capital letters and full stops.

Remember, sentences start with capital letters and end with full stops.

Write your sentences here.

Further activities
▶ Copy out the grid twice onto card. Cut out the words, keeping the two sets separate. Place the words face down on a flat surface, and take it in turns to turn them over. The aim is to collect pairs of words. The person to collect most pairs wins!

▶ Copy out the grid onto card. Cut out the words, and ask your child to make sentences by physically placing the words next to each other. Read the sentences back with your child.

In the Past

Turn the 'today' sentences into 'yesterday' sentences by changing the coloured word.

Today we play with our toys.
Yesterday we _____ with our toys.

Today she waves goodbye.
Yesterday she _____ goodbye.

Today you say, "Good morning."
Yesterday you _____, "Good morning."

Today I drink cola.
Yesterday I _____ cola.

Today he is happy.
Yesterday he _____ happy.

Today they listen to music.
Yesterday they _____ to music.

Focus These activities will teach your child about verbs in the past tense.

How to use these pages
1. With your child, read the sentences in the present tense, and then turn them into the past tense by filling in the blanks.
2. Read the page from the story on the right of this page – ask your child to read it as it is, and then to write the story in the present tense, by filling the gaps as appropriate.

Not all words in the past end with ed! Keep a close eye out for tricky ones.

Now fill in the gaps in the present tense.

There was a little girl called Ilona who had a favourite toy. It was a teddy bear whose name was Albert. One day, Ilona was playing with Albert when suddenly a hole appeared in his foot, and even bigger holes appeared in both of his hands. Ilona tried to mend them by putting a sock on his foot and gloves on his hands.

There ____ a little girl called Ilona who ____ a favourite toy. It ____ a teddy bear whose name ____ Albert. One day, Ilona ____ playing with Albert when suddenly a hole _____ in his foot, and even bigger holes _____ in both of his hands. Ilona _____ to mend them by putting a sock on his foot and gloves on his hands.

Further activities
- Read a favourite story with your child, converting it into the present tense.
- Take some pages from a book and help your child to find how many of the past tense words end with -ed.
- Ask your child to write a simple story in the past tense. Children often mix up present and past tenses when story-writing, so encourage them to think carefully as they write.

 Most stories are written in the past tense. Read *Spot goes on Holiday* by Eric Hill (Heinemann, 1989) which is written in the present tense. With your child convert it into the past tense.

Helping your child

Develop your child's writing skills

Learning to write is not just about learning letters of the alphabet or punctuation. It is about learning to communicate through the written word.

There are many ways to help your child develop his or her literacy skills:

- Help your child write lists for different purposes, e.g. shopping, holidays and parties.

- Ask your child to write letters to people, for instance, friends or relatives. It is fun to try writing to the publisher of your child's favourite author.

- Suggest your child keeps a diary of his or her life.

- Place some magnetic letters on a refrigerator or freezer door for your child to develop his or her word-building skills.

- Allow your child to practise his or her writing using a variety of media. Vary pencil and paper activities with chalkboards or a typewriter or word processor.

- Encourage your child to write words, such as his or her name, by writing over or beneath words scribed by you.

- Keep a book of words (in alphabetical order) appropriate to your child, e.g. family names, pets' names or addresses.

- Suggest your child copies out simple stories and reads them aloud to you.

- While reading stories, ask your child to pause at full stops and smile to reinforce the importance of punctuation.

These are just a few suggestions to support your child's writing. Seize any appropriate moment to show your child that opportunities to write are all around us.

But, most of all, make writing experiences positive and enjoyable. Happy children always make the best progress.

The ot Pot and the at Hat

the at hat

the ot pot

Picture word cards for 'ot' and 'at'

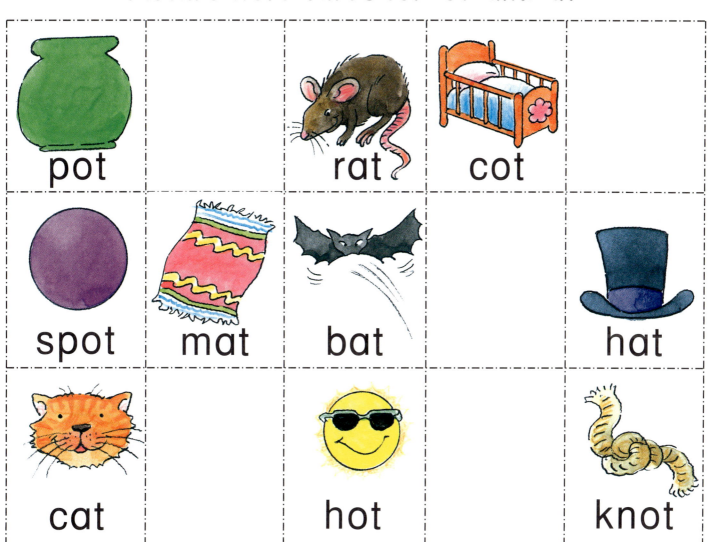

Alphabetical Houses – Picture word cards

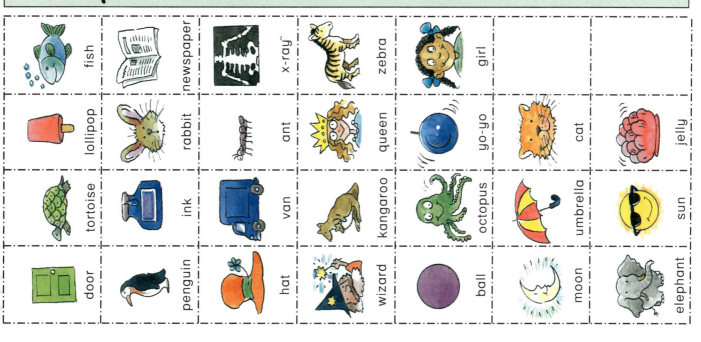

Alphabetical Houses

Castle Adventure Book

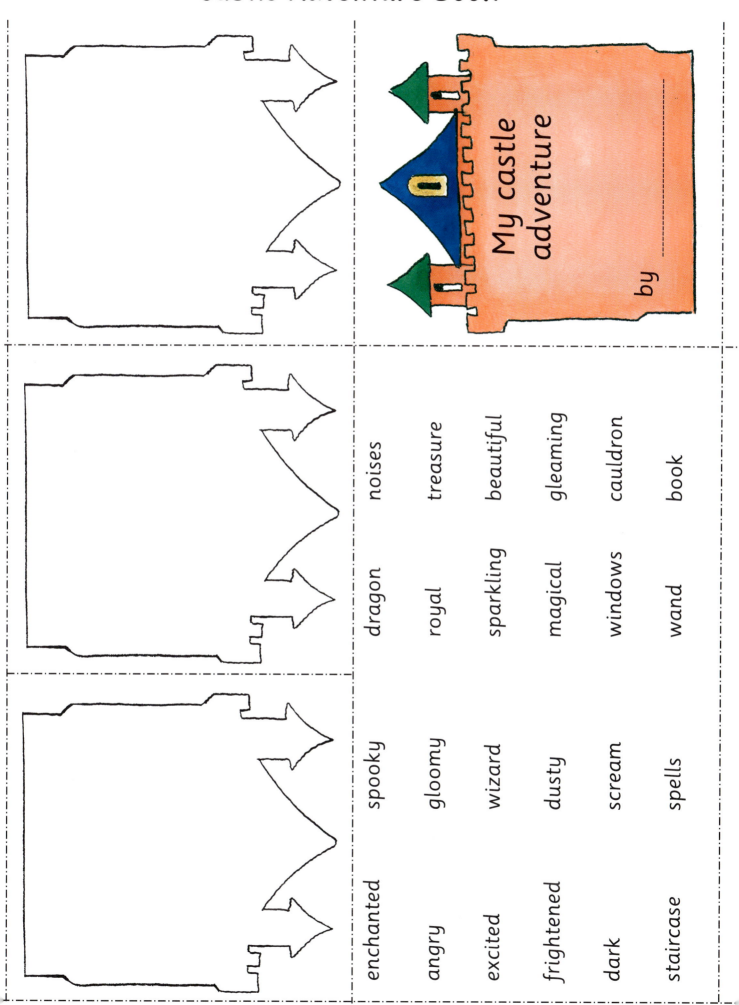